NATURE SMARTS

WORKBOOK

ALL ABOUT WATER

AGES 4–6

The Environmental
Educators of

Mass Audubon

Tia Pinney,
Kris Scopinich,
and Rina Zampieron

The mission of Storey Publishing is to serve our customers by publishing practical information that encourages personal independence in harmony with the environment.

Edited by Deanna F. Cook and Diana Rupp
Art direction and book design by Michaela Jebb
Text production by Jennifer Jepson Smith
Illustrations by © Jada Fitch

Storey Publishing
210 MASS MoCA Way
North Adams, MA 01247
storey.com

Storey Publishing is an imprint of Workman Publishing, a division of Hachette Book Group, Inc., 1290 Avenue of the Americas, New York, NY 10104. The Storey Publishing name and logo are registered trademarks of Hachette Book Group, Inc.

Distributed in Europe by Hachette Livre, 58 rue Jean Bleuzen, 92 178 Vanves Cedex, France
Distributed in the United Kingdom by Hachette Book Group, UK, Carmelite House, 50 Victoria Embankment, London EC4Y 0DZ

ISBN: 978-1-63586-780-0 (Paperback)

Printed in Canada by Transcontinental
Printing on paper from responsible sources
TC
10 9 8 7 6 5 4 3 2 1

Library of Congress Cataloging-in-Publication Data on file

CONTENTS

Water Is Everywhere

Did you know that all life on Earth needs water to survive, from the smallest insects to the tallest trees? Building your water smarts will help you learn all the ways living things need water and how we can protect our water sources for animals, plants, and people. Let's dive in!

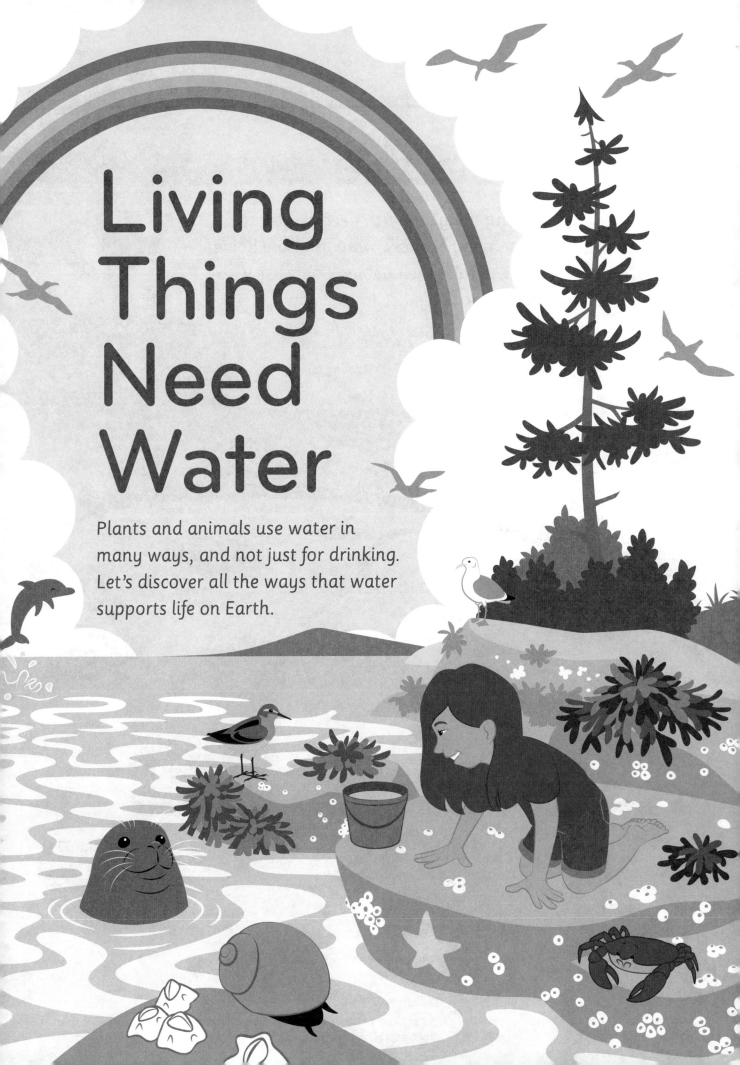

Living Things Need Water

Plants and animals use water in many ways, and not just for drinking. Let's discover all the ways that water supports life on Earth.

We All Need Water

Every living thing on Earth needs water to drink. For many animals, water is also a home or a place to raise their babies. Some use water for washing or as a place to cool down.

➤ Circle all the examples you see of a plant or animal using water.

Living
Things Need
Water

7

Answer
key on
page 93

How Animals Use Water

Animals use water in many different ways. Bathing, breathing, staying cool, and providing a home or shelter are some ways that animals use water.

➤ Follow each line from an animal to one way they use water.

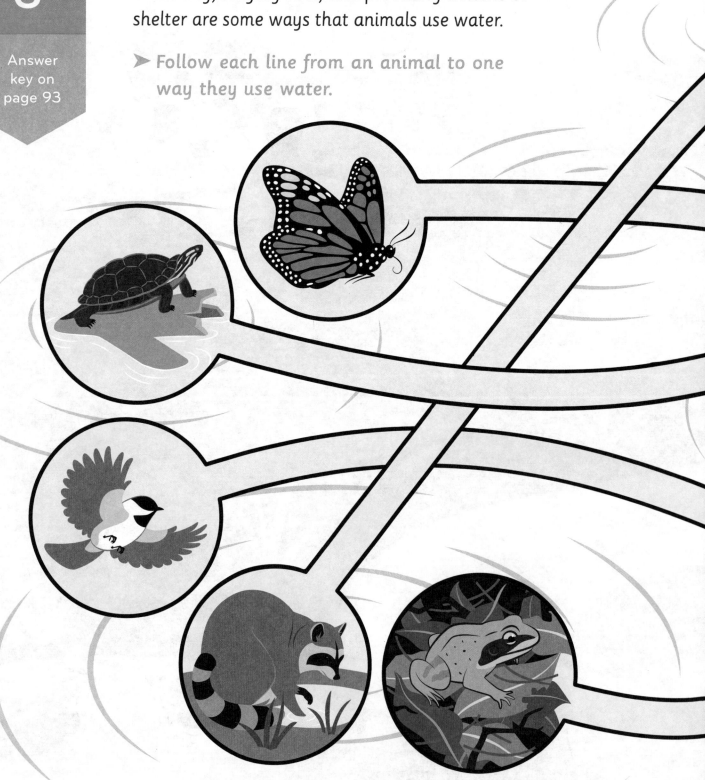

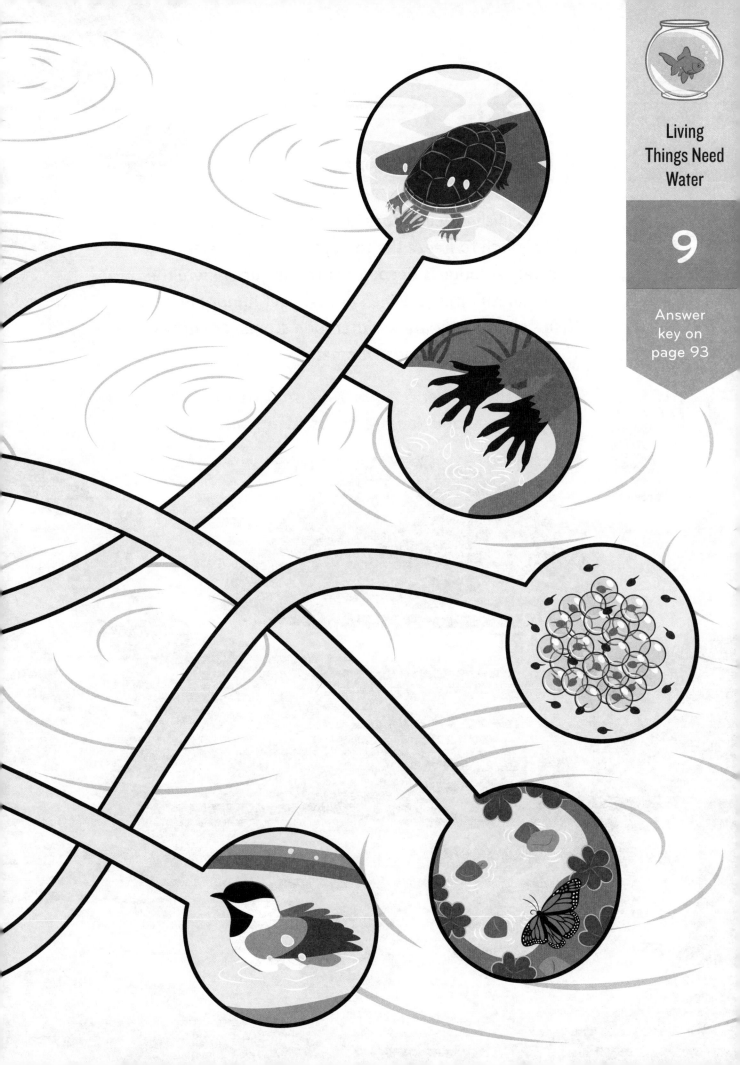

Living Things Need Water

10

Answer key on page 93

Help Feed the Beaver

Beavers live in their lodges all year long, even when it's cold enough to freeze the top of the pond. The entrance to a beaver lodge is deep under the surface where the water doesn't freeze. When beavers get hungry in winter, they swim to their underwater food stores, or caches. (Beavers are very good swimmers!)

➤ Help the beaver find its way from its lodge to its winter food (edible barks, twigs, and leaves).

START

HOME SWEET HOME

Beavers build dams in streams out of sticks, branches, mud, and rocks. The dams create deep ponds where beavers build their lodges.

FINISH

Living
Things Need
Water

12

Answer
key on
page 93

Water Ways

Animals that live in water have special body parts that help them hunt, move, hide, and more.

➤ Draw a line to match each animal to the body part that helps it in a watery world.

BEAVER
Beavers slap their tails on the water to warn their family of danger.

ALLIGATOR
Alligators can hide underwater because their eyes and nostrils are on top of their heads.

DUCK
Ducks have webbed feet that paddle smoothly through water.

NEWT
Some newts use gills for breathing in water during the earliest stages of life.

FISH
Fish scales can help with protection and be useful for camouflage.

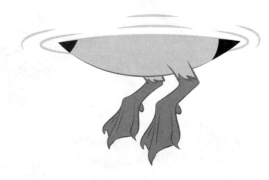

SEAL
Seals use their claws for grooming and defense.

Living
Things Need
Water

14

Answer
key on
page 93

Pond Search

➤ Check off the wetland plants and animals you find in the pond picture.

❏ Frog

❏ Dragonfly

❏ Lily pad

❏ Songbird

❏ Cattail

❏ Duck

❏ Fish

❏ Turtle

❏ Butterfly

❏ Water lily

❏ Tadpole

❏ Newt

Make a Butterfly Puddling Station

Butterflies flutter around gardens—and muddy or sandy puddles. They collect nectar (the sugary water made by plants) from gardens. And they get nutrients they need from muddy puddles. You can make a simple puddling station for the butterflies in your neighborhood.

HERE IS WHAT YOU WILL NEED.

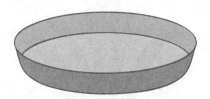

Shallow dish or container

Soil

Water

Salt

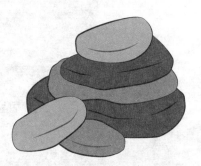

A few flat rocks

Ripe fruit (optional)

1 Fill the dish halfway with soil, add enough water to moisten the soil, and sprinkle salt on top.

2 Place some flat rocks on the soil for the butterflies to land on. If you want, add a piece or two of ripe fruit (like banana slices, strawberries, or half an orange) for the butterflies to feed on.

3 Be sure to keep the soil moist when the weather is hot or dry, which is the time butterflies are most likely to visit.

4 Observe what's happening. Do butterflies visit one at a time, or in a group? What colors do you see on the butterflies? Are they all the same type? How long do they stay?

Living
Things Need
Water

18

Answer
key on
page 94

Habitat Match-Up

A habitat is the place where a plant or animal finds shelter, food, and water. Some animals live in a water habitat. Other animals need water in their habitat to drink or lay eggs.

➤ Draw a line from each habitat to the animal that lives there.

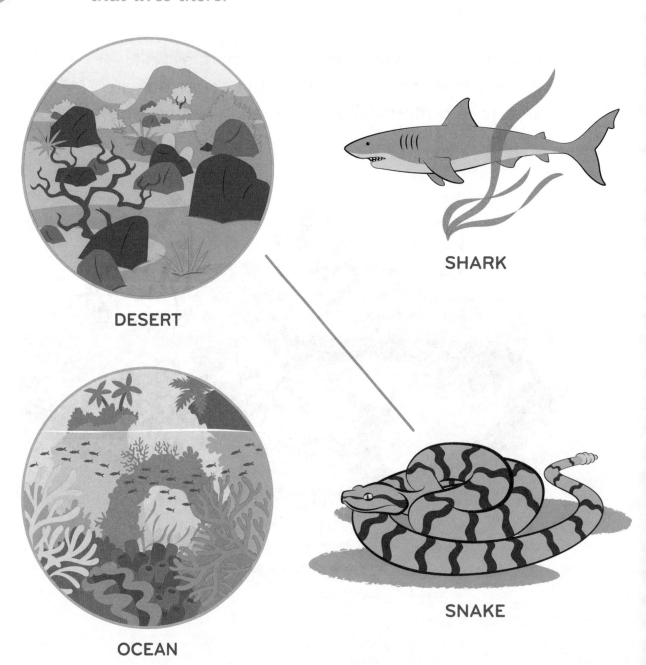

SHARK

DESERT

SNAKE

OCEAN

POND

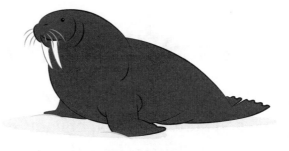

WALRUS

WETLAND

FROG

ARCTIC

MOOSE

Plants Need Water, Too

Just like animals, plants depend on water. But plants don't drink the way animals do. Instead, plants have roots that pull water from the ground so it can move all the way up into the leaves.

➤ Follow the path that water takes: from the rain that drips into the soil, travels through the tree's roots, and moves all the way out to the leaves!

START

FINISH

Living
Things Need
Water

21

Answer
key on
page 94

Watch a Plant "Breathe"

Plants absorb water through their roots and use that water to grow. Extra water is released by the leaves as water vapor. This is called **transpiration**. You can see transpiration by trying this simple experiment.

HERE IS WHAT YOU WILL NEED.

*Plant (either a houseplant in a sunny window or one in the garden)

Plastic bag

String or clothespin

*Not an evergreen or succulent

1 Place your plastic bag over a few of the leaves of your plant (or the whole plant, if it's small enough).

2 Seal the bag around the leaves (or plant) using string to tie it, or a clothespin to clip it.

3 Come back once an hour for a few hours to observe what happens inside the plastic bag. What do you see inside the bag? Do you see moisture? What do you think happens to this water when there is no bag on the plant?

4 Remember to remove the bag when you're done with the experiment!

BE A NATURE HERO

Make a Habitat

Depending on the weather or time of year, it can be hard for animals to find water. By providing water when it is in short supply, you are helping animals and being a Nature Hero. What can you do to help supply water for plants and animals in your neighborhood? Who needs it for drinking? Who needs it for bathing? Here are some suggestions.

★ Leave a pet-safe water dish outside your house. Be sure to refill it during the heat of the day!

★ Set up a cool toad home. In a shady spot, bury a terra-cotta pot on its side partway into the dirt. Include a shallow dish of water that you can refill if necessary.

★ Create a bird water station. You can make a simple free-standing birdbath for your home. Place a shallow dish on a large, upturned bucket or flowerpot. Be sure to replace the water regularly!

Draw, photograph, or write about what you did. Did any animals come to make use of your setup?

States of Water

Water is an amazing shape changer! Room-temperature water is a liquid we can drink. When water is heated, it evaporates into a gas called **steam**, or water vapor. When very cold, water freezes into a solid called **ice**. Let's learn more about how water changes between being a liquid, solid, or a gas.

FUN FACT
The word *states* describes water in its different forms: liquid, solid, or gas.

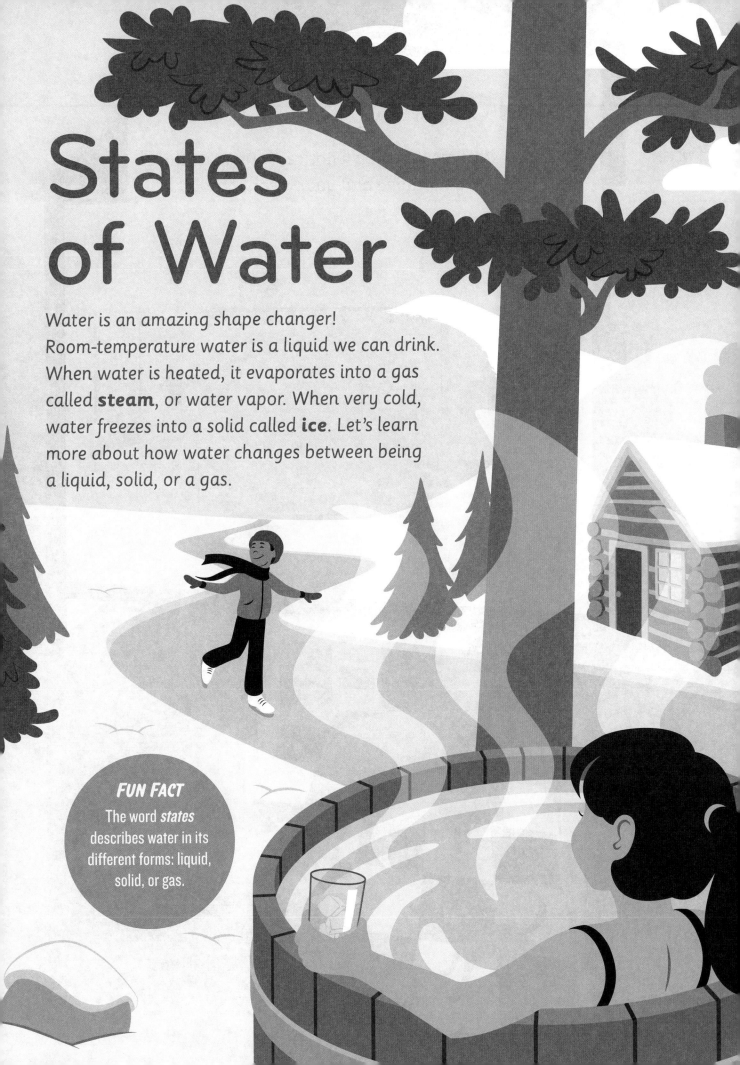

Find the Water

Once you start looking, you'll notice water in its three states around your home and your neighborhood.

WATER   ICE   WATER VAPOR

➤ Circle all of the examples of water (liquid), make a square around ice (solid), and draw a triangle around any water vapor (gas).

States
of Water

28

Water in My Home

Now it's your turn to find water (liquid, solid, and gas) where you live. You can find water in many places and states.

☐ Faucet

☐ Hose

☐ Ice cubes in a tray

☐ Steaming mug of tea

☐ Toilet

☐ Pet dish

➤ How many of these can you find or make on your own or with a grown-up? Check off each one you find.

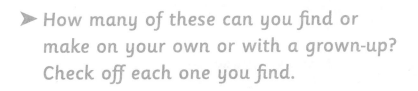

☐ Steam from a shower

☐ A full bathtub

☐ Cup of water

☐ Washing machine

☐ Steaming dryer vent

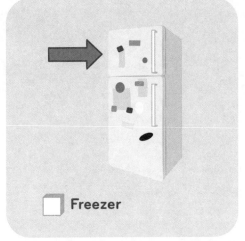

☐ Freezer

What Made the Ice "Sculpture"?

When water freezes into its solid state, it becomes the shape of the container it is frozen in. Cubes are just one of the many shapes of ice.

➤ Draw a line to match each ice "sculpture" to the container it was in when it turned to ice.

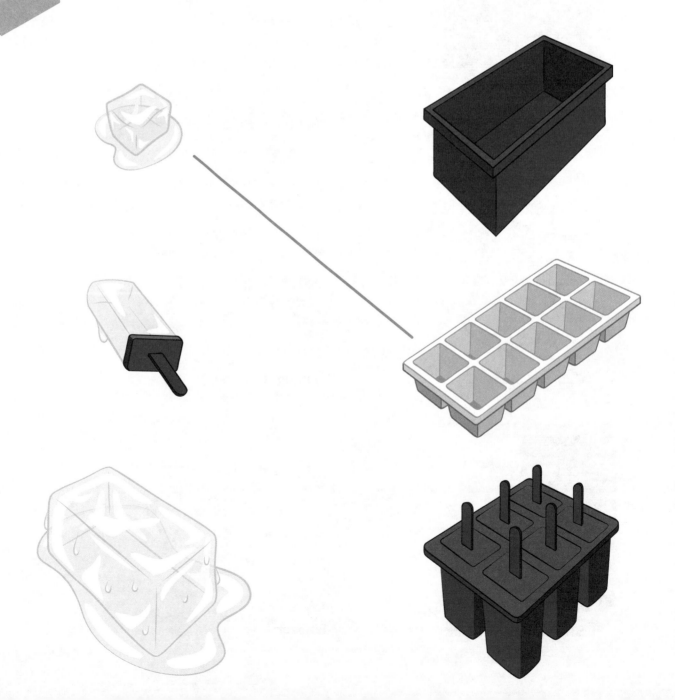

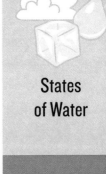

Look for unusual
objects or containers
to make your own
ice sculptures.
What shapes did
you make?

Painting with Ice

There are many ways to make art with ice. You can shape sculptures out of ice, and you can also paint with it!

HERE IS WHAT YOU WILL NEED.

Water

Ice cube tray

Food coloring

Ice-pop sticks

Aluminum foil

Thick white paper
or card stock

1 Pour water into the ice cube tray.

2 Add several drops of food coloring to each cube. Carefully stir the water in each cube with an ice-pop stick.

3 Cover the ice cube tray with foil and poke an ice-pop stick through the foil into each section. Place the tray in the freezer.

4 When the cubes are frozen, take them out and use them as paintbrushes on your paper. As the ice melts, the colors will transfer to your paper!

Thank You, Water!

We use water every day. Have you ever stopped to think how important water is to you (and all the things you love)?

➤ Using the words in the word bank, write a letter on each blank space to finish the sentences.

WORD BANK

Duck	Pond
Snowman	Shirt
Grow	Water

I use water to wash my

S _ _ _ _ .

When it rains, water helps the flowers

G _ _ _ .

When I am thirsty, I need to drink

W_____.

In hot weather, I might wade in a

P_____.

A bird with webbed feet that lives near water is a

D_____.

In winter, water can be snow or ice. My favorite thing to do with water in winter is build a

S_____.

Melting Ice Race

When it is very cold outside, puddles can turn to ice. When ice forms on roads and sidewalks, it's very slippery. Sand makes it less slippery and salt makes the ice melt.

➤ Challenge a friend or family member to see who can melt their ice cube the fastest.

HERE IS WHAT YOU WILL NEED.

Ice cubes

Cups

Die

Lamp

Salt

Warm water

➤ Give each person an ice cube in an empty cup. Take turns rolling the die and doing what the number says. Whoever melts their whole cube first wins!

Hold it for 10 counts.

Hold it up to a lamp for 10 counts.

Blow on it for 10 counts.

Leave it in the cup for 10 counts.

Put salt on it for 10 counts.

Float it in warm water for 10 counts.

Water Dot-to-Dots

In nature, water is constantly changing from solid to liquid to vapor and back again. We make water change its shape by everyday things we do.

➤ Connect the dots to discover how we can cause water to change its state.

MELT

FREEZE

States
of Water

39

STEAM

BE A NATURE HERO

No Water to Waste!

In some areas of the world, water is plentiful, and in other areas it is scarce. No matter where you live, water is always a resource we need to preserve.

We can help reduce our water use and save water. Here are some Nature Hero ideas:

★ Turn off the water when you are brushing your teeth.

★ Take a shower instead of a bath (showers use less water).

★ Use leftover water to water a plant or garden instead of pouring it down a drain.

★ Set up a family game of timing showers. Who has the fastest time?

Water Cycle

Water does more than just change its form. It travels around the world! You'll find out how water moves from oceans to clouds to rain to rivers as you learn about the amazing water cycle.

Water Color

Water collects in clouds and falls to Earth as rain or snow. Then it flows into rivers, ponds, and oceans, or soaks into the ground. Some water evaporates into gas (water vapor), rising into the sky and forming clouds. When it rains the cycle begins all over again!

➤ Color each part of the water cycle.

No Color

1 Red

2 Orange

3 Yellow

4 Light Green

5 Dark Green

6 Light Blue

7 Dark Blue

8 Purple

9 Gray

Water Cycle

43

Answer key on page 94

Water Cycle

44

Evaporation vs. Condensation

Liquid water turning into vapor is called **evaporation**. Water vapor turning back into a liquid is called **condensation**.

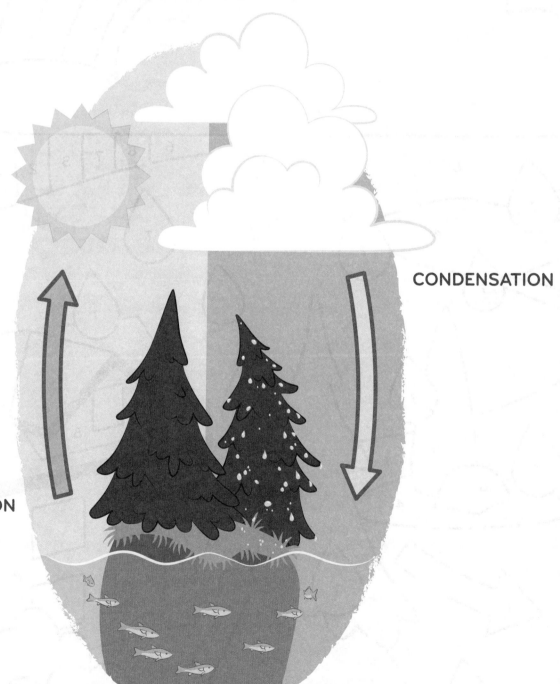

CONDENSATION

EVAPORATION

➤ Draw a cloud around pictures of evaporation
and a water drop around condensation.

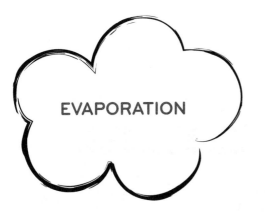

EVAPORATION

CONDENSATION

Water Cycle in a Bag

Try this fun activity to see water change from liquid to vapor and back again!

HERE IS WHAT YOU WILL NEED.

Permanent marker

Plastic sealable bag

Food coloring

Cup

Water

Spoon

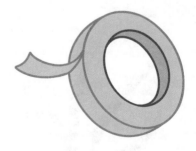

Tape

1 With your marker draw a picture of clouds and a sun on the top half of the plastic bag.

2 Mix a few drops of food coloring in a cup of water and stir. Carefully pour the water into the plastic bag. Make sure to seal the bag completely.

3 Tape the bag to the inside of a sunny window. (Be sure to use enough tape so it doesn't fall down!)

4 Visit the bag several times over the next few days. You'll notice droplets of water forming on the upper half of the plastic bag.

5 Those droplets are from water that evaporated when the sun warmed the water, then condensed back into water on the bag's surface. Hooray, you created your own water cycle!

Water Cycle

47

Where Did the Puddle Go?

The next time it rains enough to leave puddles outside, head out when the rain ends to measure a puddle. See how quickly it evaporates or absorbs into the ground.

HERE IS WHAT YOU WILL NEED.

Chalk or string

Puddle

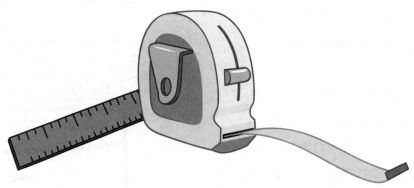

Ruler or tape measure (optional)

1   Carefully trace along the edge of the puddle with the chalk or mark it with string. Write the date and time with chalk nearby on the sidewalk or on a rock.

2   After a few hours have passed, trace the edge of the puddle again and record the time. Do this one or two more times in the next day. What do you notice about the size of the puddle? Would your puddle change size faster in sunny weather or cloudy weather?

3   Try tracing puddles on two different surfaces, such as a dirt path, paved sidewalk, or swampy field. Where does the puddle last the longest?

A Snowman in the Sun

When the sun comes out and the air warms up, snow begins to melt and will either evaporate into the air or soak into the ground.

➤ Number the pictures in order from completed snowman to what happens to the snowman when the day warms up.

Make a Rain Gauge

Try making a rain gauge to help you measure how much rain fell during a storm.

HERE IS WHAT YOU WILL NEED.

2-liter plastic bottle

Scissors

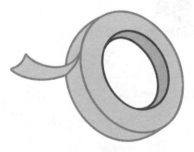

Tape

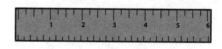

Ruler

Permanent marker

Sand or small stones (optional)

1 With an adult's help, cut off the top part of the bottle (you'll be using it in step 3). Put tape over the edges so they won't be sharp.

2 With a ruler and permanent marker, mark inches or centimeters evenly up the side of the bottle.

3 If you wish, fill the bottom of the bottle with sand or small stones to keep it from falling over in the rain. Flip the top half of the bottle upside down and slip it into the large part of the bottle. Don't forget to remove the cap!

4 Now place your gauge in a safe, flat, uncovered space outside. After the next rain, go out and check how much rain has accumulated in your gauge!

SAMPLE 1
Date and Amount of Rain Collected

_____

_____

SAMPLE 2
Date and Amount of Rain Collected

_____

_____

SAMPLE 3
Date and Amount of Rain Collected

_____

_____

Who Drank the Water?

➤ Trace each water source to the living thing that drank it.

Water Scavenger Hunt

Go for a walk and see where you notice water.
Check off each item you find.

☐ Puddle

☐ Storm runoff

☐ Clouds

☐ Dew on a car

☐ Rain

☐ Snow

☐ Dew on a spiderweb

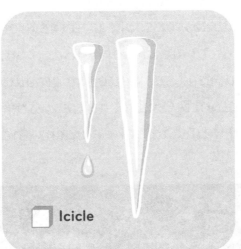

☐ Icicle

☐ Rainbow

☐ Spigot

☐ Water bottle

☐ Hose

BE A NATURE HERO

Save the Rain

After a rain, water fills up ponds and rivers, makes new puddles, or soaks into the ground. But in places where there are lots of houses, buildings, and roads, water doesn't soak into the ground as quickly. We can help nature by collecting rainwater in rain barrels and reusing it to water our gardens and plants.

Weather

Cloudy and raining, sunny and dry, cold and snowing—these are all different types of weather. Let's observe and see what weather is happening where you are right now!

Weather Report

We have many words for describing the weather, from *cloudy* or *sunny* to *snowing* or *raining*.

➤ Look at the weather pictures. Then write down today's weather report.

Weather

61

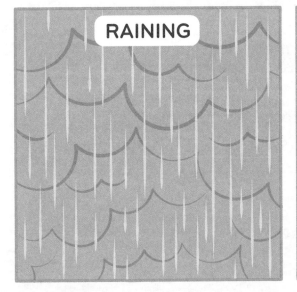

RAINING

PARTLY SUNNY

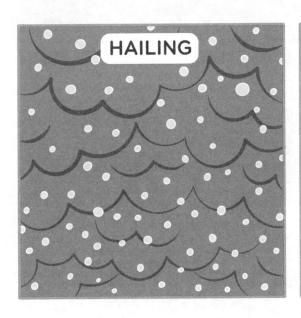

HAILING

WEATHER REPORT

TODAY'S DATE:

_____

TODAY'S WEATHER:

_____

WEATHER REPORT

TODAY'S DATE:

_____

TODAY'S WEATHER:

_____

WEATHER REPORT

TODAY'S DATE:

_____

TODAY'S WEATHER:

_____

Raindrop Math

Do you know how clouds are formed? Floating water droplets in the air join together to make clouds.

➤ Count the items in each group. Add them together, then write the answer.

5 water drops + 3 water drops = _____

1 water drop + 3 water drops = _____

4 clouds + 6 clouds =

- - - - - - - - - - -

3 rain clouds + 3 rain clouds =

- - - - - - - - - - -

Cloud Watching

Clouds can have many different shapes, textures, and even colors!

CIRRUS
thin, wispy clouds

CUMULUS
puffy, cotton ball clouds

STRATUS
thick, blanketlike
clouds

NIMBUS
dark rain or snow clouds
and thunderheads

➤ Go outside and draw the clouds you see.

Weather

66

Cotton Ball Clouds

Try your hand at making cotton ball clouds that look like the clouds you just learned about.

HERE IS WHAT YOU WILL NEED.

Glue

Cotton balls

Blue construction
paper

Gray paint

➤ Using small amounts of glue, arrange cotton ball clouds on your blue paper. You can try to form a few specific types of clouds or go wild and make up some of your own. Here are some ideas.

CIRRUS CLOUDS:
Pinch the sides of a cotton ball between two fingers and gently pull apart. Roll between your hands to make a thin, feathery shape.

CUMULUS CLOUDS:
Glue big puffy cotton balls close to each other.

NIMBUS CLOUDS:
Paint your cotton balls gray, then arrange like cumulus clouds.

STRATUS CLOUDS:
Gently pull a few cotton balls so they become thinner, but still puffy.

Weather Scavenger Hunt

You can find clues about what's happening with the weather all around you. Go outside and see how many you can find.

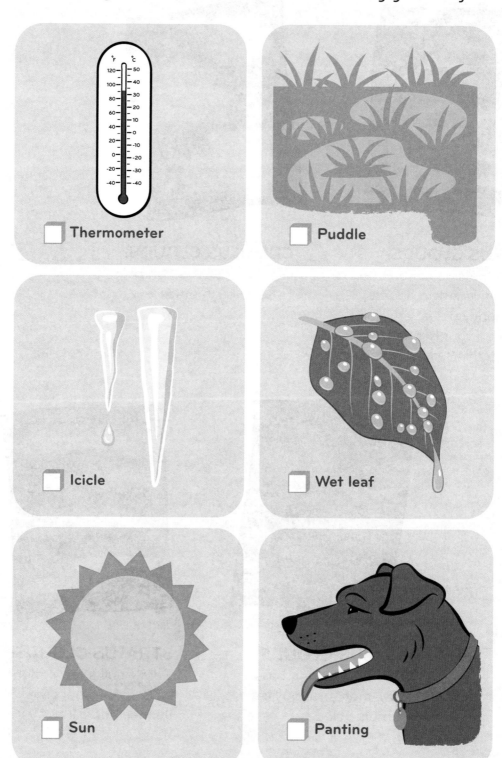

☐ Thermometer

☐ Puddle

☐ Icicle

☐ Wet leaf

☐ Sun

☐ Panting

☐ Umbrella

☐ Piled-up snow

☐ Breath on a cold day

☐ Wind

☐ Rumbling thunder

☐ Cloud

Frosty Paintings

Frost forms when the air is cold and water vapor freezes on cold windows and other surfaces. You can make your own "frosty" paintings even if you don't have cold weather.

HERE IS WHAT YOU WILL NEED.

Epsom salt

Heat-safe bowl or mug

Boiling water

Spoon

Paintbrush

Dark construction paper

1 Put ½ cup of Epsom salt into a heat-safe bowl or mug.

2 Have a grown-up pour ½ cup of boiling water into the bowl and stir until the salt is fully dissolved.

3 Let the water cool a bit so it's just warm. Dip your paintbrush into the water and brush it on the paper. As the mixture dries, the salt will crystalize on the paper. (Hint: Don't soak the paper! Light brushstrokes and simple shapes work best.)

What Do You Wear?

We dress differently depending on the weather.

➤ In each group, cross out the clothing item that you would not wear for the weather.

SUNNY

RAINING

SNOWING

BE A NATURE HERO

Climate is long-term patterns in the weather, and our climate is changing. To learn about the impact of our changing climate on plants and animals, scientists need our help. Below are a few projects kids can join to contribute to community science databases studying the impact of changing weather patterns on our world.

Search online for the environmental organizations below.

★ Nature's Notebook

★ Budburst

★ IceWatch

FUN FACT

Phenology is the timing of seasonal events such as egg laying, flowering, migration, and hibernation. These events are influenced by the climate.

Water around the World

Ocean water can be very cold or very warm but it is always salty. Fresh water flows in rivers and streams or is still in ponds and lakes. No matter what kinds of water you have near you, water is important in every corner of our planet.

Bodies of Water

Not all bodies of water are the same. In nature, water can be fresh or salty, still or moving. Some water is frozen, until it melts and turns into liquid water again.

➤ Look at the bodies of water shown. Then fill in the rest of each word using the words in the word bank.

WORD BANK

Pond   River
Oceans   Iceberg

The largest bodies of water are

O_____ _____ ____.

Fresh water that moves downhill is called a

R_____.

FUN FACT
Areas where water naturally collects are called *bodies of water*. Ponds, rivers, and lakes are all examples of bodies of water.

When fresh water is still and surrounded by land, we call it a

P_ _ _ _.

A piece of glacier that breaks off and floats on the ocean is an

I_ _ _ _ _ _ _ _.

Water around the World

78

Answer
key on
page 96

Tide Maze

If you've ever been to a beach, then you might have noticed that the ocean rises and falls along the shore. Depending on the time of day and which part of the earth is facing the moon, you can have high tide, where the water comes up high on the beach, or low tide, where the water is farther down the beach.

➤ A sea star was trapped when the high tide went out. Help the sea star make its way through the tide pools to return to the ocean.

START

FUN FACT
Low tide is an awesome time to explore because many sea creatures can be found in tide pools (puddles of ocean water trapped in the rocks until the next high tide).

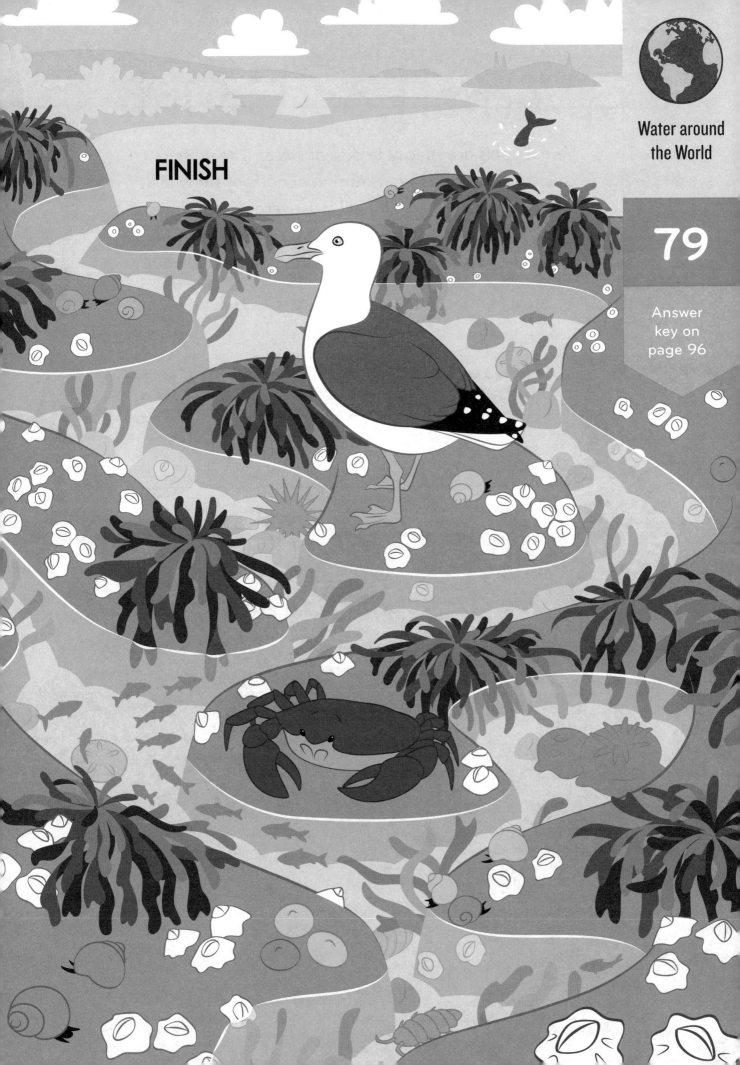

Vernal Pool Count

Vernal pools are special bodies of water. The water collects in low-lying areas during periods of snow melt and rain in spring, and by fall most vernal pools have completely dried up! There are many animals and plants that can live and reproduce only in these special pools.

➤ Look at the picture and count the creatures who live in the vernal pond.

HOW MANY TADPOLES?	HOW MANY FROGS?	HOW MANY SALAMANDERS?

Answer key on page 96

Does It Float?

Salt water and fresh water are different in more ways than how they taste. In these next two activities, you will observe more differences between salt water and fresh water.

HERE IS WHAT YOU WILL NEED.

2 glasses

Water

2 eggs

Salt

Spoon

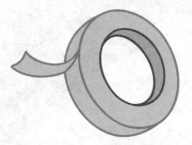

Tape

Pen or marker

1 Fill both glasses about three-quarters full with water.

2 Place one of the eggs in the first glass and notice what happens. Did the egg sink or float?

3 Add 3 tablespoons of salt to the second glass and stir until well dissolved. Add the other egg to this glass. What did you notice? Was the result the same as the first glass? If it was different, why do you think it was different?

4 Label the glasses with tape. Based on the experiment, which one is fresh water and which one is salt water? Use your pen to write your answer on the label on each glass. You can also write it on the labels in the picture below.

Celery Experiment

Plants that grow by an ocean (salt water) are different than those that grow around ponds, lakes, and rivers (fresh water). This experiment will help you see what happens when freshwater plants try to grow in salt water.

HERE IS WHAT YOU WILL NEED.

2 glasses

Water

Salt

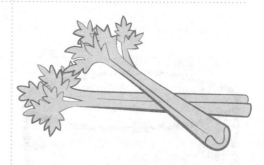

2 stalks of celery

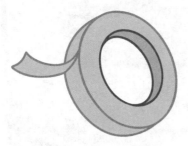

Tape

Pen or marker

1 Fill both glasses about three-quarters full with water.

2 Add 3 tablespoons of salt to one glass.

3 Place a stalk of celery in each glass. Wait a full day and check the celery stalks. Do they look the same? Is one softer than the other? Which would you rather eat?

4 Label the glasses with tape. Based on your experiment, which one is fresh water and which is salt water? Use the pen to write your answer on the label on each glass. You can also write it on the labels in the picture below.

FUN FACT
Plants that live in or near salt water have special ways of managing the high amount of salt. One type of mangrove tree even stores the extra salt in dead leaves to get rid of it!

Water near Me

No matter where you live, there is water nearby. So head outside and find a water body (pond, river, ocean, stream, swamp, or lake) near your home. Visit your water body two or three times. On each visit, notice how animals, plants, or people use the water body (a bathing spot for birds, a fun place for people to gather, a source of water for plants and animals).

➤ Draw a picture of a water body near you.

➤ Write down what you notice about the water body.

_____

_____

_____

_____

_____

➤ Every time you visit your water body,
take photos, make notes, or draw pictures.

When Do You Get Wet?

Depending on where you live, you may get a lot of rain or snow or not much at all. Each area of the US gets a different amount of rain or snow, and some seasons are wetter than others.

➤ Read what each child has to say about the rain or snow where they live.

"My name is Manuel and I live in **MIAMI**. I always take my umbrella when I go out to play in **SUMMER**. You just never know when it might start to rain!"

"I'm Tamara and I live in **BOSTON**. We get rain or snow pretty much **ALL FOUR SEASONS** of the year, so I always have my boots nearby."

"Malala here. It's pretty warm and dry all summer in **LOS ANGELES**. But in **WINTERTIME**, you better be ready to get wet!"

➤ When does it rain or snow in each place? Circle the season or seasons.

MIAMI

Winter   Spring   Summer   Fall

BOSTON

Winter   Spring   Summer   Fall

LOS ANGELES

Winter   Spring   Summer   Fall

WHERE YOU LIVE

Winter   Spring   Summer   Fall

Rainfall and Habitats

The amount of rain that falls in an area determines what types of plants can live there. Areas that get a lot of rain tend to have lots of green, leafy plants, while areas that get little rain tend to have more grasses and plants with smaller leaves.

➤ Write the numbers 1 to 4 to put the habitats in order from most rain to least.

PLAINS

1

SWAMP

DESERT

MOUNTAINS

BE A NATURE HERO

Help protect bodies of water in your area by becoming a Nature Hero. See how many items on the checklist you can complete. The more you check off, the more you are helping keep our waterways clean for animals, plants, and people.

☐ Try to walk, bike, or take a bus or train when you can, rather than use a car.

☐ Always pick up your pet waste and dispose of it in the trash.

☐ Let a grown-up know if a faucet in your home is dripping or leaking.

☐ Do not pour paint or other pollutants down your sinks or toilets.

☐ Compost your yard and garden waste so it doesn't go down storm drains.

☐ Have a trash pickup day around your neighborhood or schoolyard.

Tally it up

You get 2 points for doing each task. Earn your title!

☐ 0–2: **Cloud Catcher**

☐ 3–4: **Junior Puddle Jumper**

☐ 5–6: **Water Saver**

☐ 7–8: **Water Friend**

☐ 9–10: **Water Protector**

☐ 11–12: **Nature Hero**

Answer Key

PAGES 6–7

PAGES 8–9

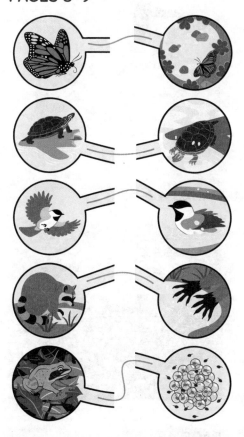

PAGES 10–11

PAGES 12–13

BEAVER

ALLIGATOR

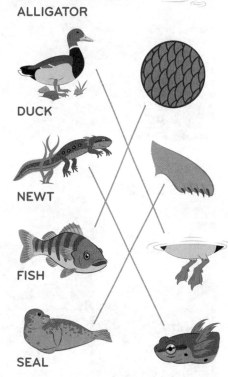

DUCK

NEWT

FISH

SEAL

PAGES 14–15

PAGES 18–19

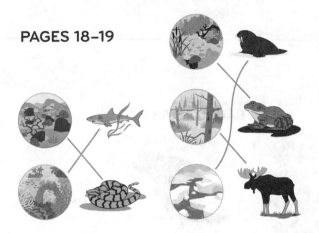

PAGES 20–21

PAGES 26–27

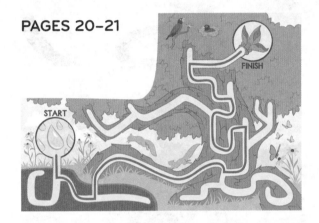

PAGES 30–31

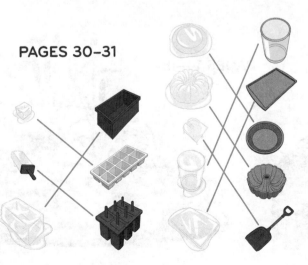

PAGES 34–35

I use water to wash my

Shirt.

When it rains, water helps flowers

Grow.

When I am thirsty, I need to drink

Water.

In hot weather, I might wade in a

Pond.

A bird that has webbed feet
and lives near water is a

Duck.

In the winter, water can be snow
or ice. My favorite thing to do
with water in winter is build a

Snowman.

PAGES 42–43

PAGE 45

PAGES 50–51

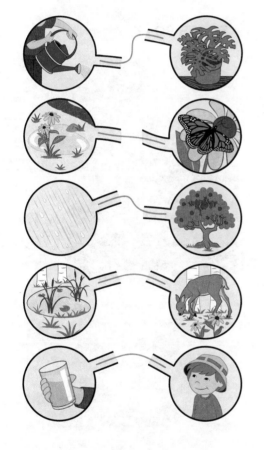

PAGES 54–55

PAGES 62–63

$$5 \text{ water drops} + 3 \text{ water drops} = 8$$

$$1 \text{ water drop} + 3 \text{ water drops} = 4$$

PAGES 72–73

SUNNY

RAINING

SNOWING

$$4 \text{ clouds} + 6 \text{ clouds} = 10$$

$$3 \text{ rain clouds} + 3 \text{ rain clouds} = 6$$

PAGES 76–77

The largest bodies of water are

O c e a n s .

Fresh water that moves downhill is called a

R i v e r .

When fresh water is still and surrounded by land, we call it a

P o n d .

A piece of glacier that breaks off and floats on the ocean is an

I c e b e r g .

PAGES 78–79

PAGES 80–81

HOW MANY TADPOLES?	HOW MANY FROGS	HOW MANY SALAMANDERS?
15	4	4

PAGES 88–89

MIAMI
Winter   Spring   (Summer)   Fall

BOSTON
(Winter   Spring   Summer   Fall)

LOS ANGELES
(Winter)   Spring   Summer   Fall

PAGES 90–91

3 PLAINS

1 SWAMP

4 DESERT

2 MOUNTAINS